A LOSS OF PRIVACY: THE GOOGLE EPIDEMIC

By *Robert Valvasori*

Professor of course in which this assignment was assigned:
Professor Olena Kobzar
Teaching Assistant for course in which this assignment was assigned:
Mr. Behzad Mohammadi
Course code for course in which this assignment was assigned:
AP/LASO 3365 6.0
Name of course in which assignment was assigned:
Privacy and the Law

Preface

Online privacy has become a major concern for people in today's society. We as users can no longer assume that information placed on the Internet by us is completely secure, especially considering world events and groups such as Edward Snowden and the Anonymous hacking group. While taking the course Privacy and the Law, it was discussed how corporations partake in selling personal information to third parties, sometimes to the dismay of users using the corporations online services. This is especially true for corporations such as Facebook, Twitter, Instagram, and Google. This entire entity was an assignment created for the course AP/LASO 3365 Privacy and the Law 6.0 and Google's privacy policy was chosen for a case study because it has played a significant role in many people's lives, and I was interested in researching the search engine's policy, as I did not know a lot about it. The assignment entailed the following:

> This essay assignment is worth 20%, and consists of an extended analysis of the privacy policy you have described in the previous assignment. In this extended analysis, you will examine in detail some of the privacy concerns that may have been raised about the social media or search engine you are studying. You will also look at whether the policy is compliant with domestic laws and international laws and treaties regarding data privacy. For this part of the essay you have to research official privacy policies such as Canada's PIPEDA and its enforcement mechanisms. Finally, in this extended analysis you will discuss any other safeguards that could be implemented to protect privacy of online users. Expect to write 10-15 pages for this component of the research paper. The second part of the essay is due May 7.

Due to Google's private policy changing from time to time, the version of Google's Private Policy I used for the assignment was the December 19, 2014 edition, which can be found at http://www.google.com/policies/privacy/. This assignment holds some significance, as it highlights the importance and the need of studying privacy in the legal sphere. Additionally, this assignment highlights the need for learning about privacy rights, as many people are unaware of the all the risks involved in sharing their information online, even after they read the terms of service (including the private policy) of a product offered by a corporation. It is my hope that this book will help create a need for more research in this field.

I would like to conclude this preface by thanking a few people that have helped me throughout this papers creation. The first are a few of my friends Sandra Odisho, Angelica Lu and Doug Mackenzie, who helped edit my first drafts of this assignment. The next person I would like to thank is the professor I had for the course; if it wasn't for her, this assignment wouldn't have been written. I also appreciated her help looking over my paper to make improvements. Finally, I would like to thank my TA. Not only did he look over this assignment to make sure I was on the right track, but also fostered a conducive environment for me to excel in my coursework.

Table of Contents

Introduction

Search engines today have helped us stay informed at continually faster speeds than ever before, with Google being one of the most popular in use. This increase in information has helped shape how we see the world around us economically, socially, and environmentally. While events such as 9/11 and potential other terrorist activities concerns the state and citizens in finding a balance between insuring security while also maintaining civil liberties, the recent revelations by Edward Snowden alarms citizens in the changing nature of the state towards becoming a security and surveillance state. Increasingly, more people are concerned with keeping information and data private. However, because of the way terrorists threats are presented in a dichotomy between security and privacy, public's expectations of privacy rights are ever changing. Increasingly more citizens are becoming more comfortable with giving up their personal information in exchange for a perceived sense of security. In response various government around the world attempt to legislate privacy policies in an attempt to both allow the government to collect and use citizens' information as well to some extent protect those information from wrongful use. Bill C-51 (discussed in depth in Appendix E) is a controversial piece of legislation that allows the government to spy on citizens suspected of terrorism (by any means necessary), without the knowledge of the citizenry. Legislation such as Canada's Personal Information Protection and Electronic Documents Act (PIPEDA) and the European Union's (EU) legislation (e.g. the Right to be Forgotten), in theory were created and intended to protect our rights online, but upon closer examination, both legislations are inadequate when being implemented to safeguard our privacy rights, especially when taking into consideration Bill C-51's effect and private policies effects on people.

In this paper I intend to assess the privacy policy of Google and evaluate whether PIPEDA is able or useful in protecting the privacy of individual users. This paper will examine how different theoretical and philosophical frameworks affect and continue to affect Google's private policy (GPP), such as privacy rights of the dead and data double. Collection of consent under the GPP will also be reviewed to examine how they affect privacy rights and if this collection decreases these rights. A question that will be considered is: can inputted data be construed as being nude, and what (if any) implications occur when the GPP is being considered. This essay will seek to prove Google's Private Policy is useless in protecting the users[1] (our) privacy rights due to the policy having many ambiguities and conditions through its phrasing, which leaves a majority of the public's private data mined by companies, sold to third parties, and/or is made public.

Privacy – the familiar stranger

Before going into more depth into this assignment, it is important to first discuss the concept of privacy. For millennia, the concept of privacy has changed from society to society, and from time period to time period. This can be attributed to the change of ideas and that the concept of privacy is a social construction (no one definition for privacy exists, even though it appears obvious). Due to this fluidity, it is difficult to expect corporations to implement safeguards and it would be difficult for states to establish and implement a definition for privacy, along with regulating it (Carucci, 130-1). Although an imperfect definition, a basic framework definition of privacy as a right (specifically an internet privacy right) that will be used for this paper is "freedom from damaging publicity, public scrutiny, secret surveillance, or unauthorized disclosure of one's personal data or information, as by a government, corporation, or individual(s)", while privacy in of itself will be defined as "the state of being free from unwanted or undue intrusion or disturbance in one's private life or affairs; freedom to be let alone", as many people may consider this an underlying tenant of defining what privacy and privacy rights

---

[1] See Appendix C on page 21 for more context.

means to them (Keizer, 14-9). A drawback of using these definitions though is that they can be considered too narrow in their scope for some people, while too broad for others. Just because no definitive definition exists for privacy should not discourage research, but encourage it, as further research on the subject will not only promote more discussion, but also "maintain 'our very integrity as persons'" if "privacy has to do with our essential humanity" (Keizer, 22-3).

The Law and Privacy Protection

Under examination of both PIPEDA and GPP, it appears Google is compliant with Canadian privacy laws. It also appears that Google exploits a few of PIPEDA's principles through loopholes. The first issue transpires with accountability – at the time of this paper's completion, there was no contact information contained in the main section of GPP to contact Google's privacy officer (GPO) if we (the 'users') ever had a concern with private information stored in Google's servers, even though GPP promises users access to their information if they need it (with some exceptions) [Kobzar, Lecture 12]. This is problematic for two reasons: (i) with the contact info for GPO it is hard to find for users, which makes it difficult to hold Google accountable for actions that users perceive to be violating their rights; and (ii) one of the exceptions to the user's access to personal information are harmful to user's privacy rights – users are not allowed to change or delete their information if they are keeping it "for legitimate business or legal purposes". It poses risks because (a) we do not know what a "legitimate business purpose" is or what it entails; (b) users do not know what standards Google uses to determine what information is given/considered for "legal purposes"; (c) GPP does not specify if users are informed if their personal information was accessed by law enforcement or by another agency for "legitimate business purposes"; (d) Google does not always have the ability to remove information on users due to information being stored in other countries (i.e. the information stored is subjected to different laws); and (e) Google does not know how accurate or reflective information it collects is, which can be harmful to users because people may be arrested for what they searched without a proper explanation given by the 'user'. An example of this is a professor getting arrested for their Google search history if it was found out they were supposedly doing an illegal act (e.g. child pornography), even though the reason for the supposedly illegal act was for conducting their research to get a better understanding of a problem (Kobzar, Lecture 12).

Issues dealing with consent are at the heart of the next issue (Kobzar, Lecture 12). Unlike companies like Apple that require the user to "accept" their terms and conditions, Google employs an implicit consent platform. This means that a user automatically accepts Google's conditions when they use the company's products. This is problematic because it does not give a real choice to users to choose what they wish to share with others. Furthermore, it is the user's responsibility to inform themselves of the GPP, not Google's, which is problematic because giving choice to users to not read the policy runs the risk of users losing more private information than they originally intended. Additionally, Google does not know if the user is capable of understanding its terms and/or able to give consent (e.g. some mentally-ill persons and/or young children). This is problematic because if users do not know what they are agreeing to, it may reduce their privacy (due to giving up more information), which can pose risks in their later life (e.g. not being able to get a job because of a user's search history, or a person might not be able to get medical insurance because their medical history was put on the web) [Solove, 4-5]. Google does not readily specify how long it retains the data it collects, it does not give specifics on how they delete/remove personal data, and it does not give a guarantee that it will delete all personal data about a user from its servers (Kobzar, Lecture 12). This is problematic because: (i) should a hacker wish to steal personal information on multiple users, they can if the personal data is stored on the company's systems long enough and/or if the company's online security is weak; and (ii) personal information on users could potentially remain on Google's servers forever, which poses the question of why does a company like Google need to keep data on the deceased or dead. A precarious situation that stems from point one as well is that users may not be informed that a company was hacked (the company may hide it to maintain users trust), which can increase risks for information users choose to and/or have to put on the internet. Another potential problem is data mining – although data is anonymously collected, with the right research, it would not be difficult to identify someone (or their location) by using tracking features (e.g. "cookies") to isolate and find a specific user (Kobzar, Lecture 12). This may be problematic to users because they could be bombarded with ads that are irrelevant, annoying, and/or disturbing. The last issue at the time of this paper's writing lies with the problem of notifying people that GPP exists - it is up to most users to search for GPP to inform themselves of the information contained in the policy and must check regularly should any changes occur in it (Kobzar, Lecture 12). This is problematic because it allows Google to profit off of data mining information from its uninformed users (in most cases unfortunately, most people fall into the category of 'uninformed users'); that is to say that Google exploits peoples' apathy to read and inform themselves to policies that could potentially harm them (releasing information that users may wish to remain private).

For PIPEDA to be more effective in closing loopholes in GPP, a few changes need to occur. The first is to pressure companies to make clear what constitutes "legitimate business purposes" when keeping data on users, so users can be better informed on what information they reveal on the internet. Secondly, companies should be required under the Act to provide clear private policies that inform users what threshold is required for law enforcement to be allowed to take data from these companies. Stemming from these two ideas is getting PIPIEDA to insist that companies provide concrete, simple to understand policies, which users will actually understand (e.g. elaborating on parts of private policies that have "can" and "may" so that users better understand what they are agreeing too). Thirdly, PIPEDA should require companies to include all relevant information about privacy in their private policy. This is important because it would give users a better understanding of the policy without needing to click on multiple links, and it would give easier access to crucial information such as the contact information of GPO so that users can report if a potential violation occurred, or to be better informed. Additionally, it would hold Google responsible should something happen. Fourthly, PIPEDA should stipulate that companies should create a test for users to be administered occasionally to assess a user's knowledge of the specific company's private policy. If a user gets less than a certain amount, then they would not be able to be use the website. This would be beneficial to users of Google, as it would inform users of what information Google protects and/or releases. Furthermore it would educate users enough to limit what information they are willing to share. Lastly, PIPEDA should be changed so that companies would be required to put everything related to their privacy policy in one document, so users have easier access to specific relevant information, such as how long their information is retained/stored and if (and how) their information is deleted. This would be important, as it would limit what information users decide to input online.

As of May 13th, 2014, an EU court upheld a concept of the right to be forgotten ("Factsheet on the 'Right to be Forgotten' ruling [C131-12]"). The concept shows promise because it forces search engines to delete "inaccurate, inadequate or excessive" links about a person when a user requests it, under certain conditions, and the court ruled that in particular cases, "a person's right to data protection could not be justified merely by the economic interest of the search engine" ("Factsheet on the 'Right to be Forgotten' ruling [C131-12]"). This is significant, as it shifts some responsibility to Google to maintain some secrecy for users information it collects, stores and/or uses. Unfortunately, there are a few problems with this right: (i) it is not absolute because a balance exists with individual's online "private" life verses "the interest of the public in having access to that information" and "information needs to be 'outdated' before compliance of a takedown request is done"; and (ii) information people ask to be removed in the EU cannot permanently be deleted due to how information is transferred from different areas of the internet [information on a website can copied to another, with both being in separate countries/continents] ("Factsheet on the 'Right to be Forgotten' ruling [C131-12]"; Baker). The second reason means that the EU's laws are not applicable to an EU user's information that has been transferred to a non EU country (e.g. the United States) due to jurisdictional restriction and trade deal issues. This can be seen with the *Safe Harbor Agreement*[2] the EU has with the US, in which certain people's privacy rights are beached in the name of national security to prevent "terrorism" (e.g. those in the EU travelling to the US are subject to disclosing certain information to 'prove' they are not a threat) [Heisenberg, 1-13].

Two questions that arise include (i) should Canada consider adopting a similar "right to be forgotten" law, and (ii) is the EU's law better than PIPEDA or vice versa? The answer to the first question is that we could consider it because the law is a useful tool for users to keep their privacy, but before we as a nation consider it, the right to be forgotten law must be tweaked so as to better protect user's privacy rights. This includes: (i) make rulings based on harm done instead of relying on the vagueness of what constitutes "outdated" or "irrelevant" information to allow more consistency in cases; (ii) form an agreement with Google so it is obligated to delist

---

[2] See Appendix A on page 19 for more details on this Agreement.

information from all domains it controls to grant users greater access to privacy; and (iii) create a guide for the public that is accessible and straightforward on what under the law is considered private, what is considered the public's right to know, and what private corporations and the state have access to (Baker). The third reason is significant because it raises an issue – who is responsible for private information online? This is important because it establishes who is (or should be) responsible for privacy dilemma. The question of who is responsible lies with three entities: the state, us, or companies. The state cannot take full responsibility because it would overstep its jurisdictions with other countries, and the state should not be held responsible for the imprudence of some citizens. Governments should not overstep it boundaries because should they do so, they could be compared to authoritative regiments, on the grounds that they would have the potential to block and eliminate material they do not like (similar to countries like China). Corporations should not be fully held responsible for the piffle of some citizens, because a lot of information is given by them purposely, but at the same token, these companies should have some obligation to keep extremely sensitive information (e.g. credit card information) secret to maintain the trust of users. Users should not take full responsibility because many internet websites require personal information before their use or collect information due to either "implied" or forceful consent (often times without the user knowing), which can be seen as a problem because these corporations could sell this data to other parties, which can harm a person's future life. The importance of the last two points is that it recognizes that humans are social animals that require some clear structure before doing an action, while also recognizing that there are consequences to those actions. Based on this information, one comes to the conclusion that none of these groups should be responsible at the singular level, but should be responsible on the collective level. This means that the state, the corporation (Google in this case), and the user should be sharing responsibility on how best to handle privacy issues. This can be done in a few ways: (i) at the state level, laws can be made or changed so that they are not broad enough that privacy will no longer exist, while also not making them strict enough that legitimate business endeavours can still thrive; (ii) at the corporate level, make a means so that users have more access to privacy, even if that means having to create an international agreement and/or get a user to pay for the service instead of getting it for free; and (iii) at the user level, get readers to inform themselves of what corporations are allowed to take and store, while also setting a practise that users do not post information online unless they absolutely need to. Although these points are ideal and should be in place, the likelihood of them actually being implemented fully is improbable because of the amount of money corporations are making from this data and people are probably not going to share less on the internet because we perceive free services as more beneficial to us then our privacy rights[3]. The answer to the second main question is that neither are better than each other; if anything, they are both similar – they both have an inability to protect peoples 'privacy rights' 100 percent of the time due to how much information people share (and have access to) and how this information is stored, used, and removed.

Exploring Implications of GPP

Information Google collects can be problematic because (i) ads generated can become overbearing, repetitive, inappropriate, or give Google more information about a user than the user intends (e.g. age); and (ii) Google is allowed to know what device is being used to access its cite, which gives Google information on location of a user (e.g. when Google accesses a phone number, the area code can tell Google the approximate location of a user, while Wi-Fi access can give an even better approximation), the socio-economic status of a person (if Google sees that a

---

[3] See Appendix F on page 25

user is accessing its cite from an I-phone, it may indicate that the user has a lot of money and may be willing to spend more money on Google, versus a user accessing Google from a lower-ended computer). GPP does not specifically tell users who are Google's partners, they must click on a link for it. This is problematic because user's will not usually be inclined to click it, due to either not wanting to read even more than they need to or not having enough time in their lives to inform themselves of each of the 'partners' and their private policies. In the "How we use information that we collect" section, Google states it uses collected information to 'protect' its services, which is a problem because it does not specifically specify how that is done, or why it is relevant to have in the policy. In this same section, Google mentions that if other users have the original users e-mail and/or other identifying information, Google may show them more information, which is problematic because the additional information may be used to indirectly discriminate against the original user (e.g. if someone's full name is released to a company, it could associate them to a particular religion, which may prevent a user from being employed due to associating them with terrorism). Although race, religion, sexual orientation, and health are supposedly protected from tailored ads, in reality they are not. For example, if a user searches up a medical condition and possible cures for it (e.g. surgery or consuming certain foods/pills), Google Ads may pick up on this and advertise certain products or lifestyles to help 'cure' their problem, thus eliminating the user's privacy. Another problem presented by GPP is the storage and processing of a user's data. According to the policy, both these processes may be done outside a user's home country, which is problematic because personal information is subject to the new country's laws, not the user's home country. This issue affects users, because they could be barred from entering another country, or be added to a terrorism list because of the information was collected and stored under different laws (this issue gained international attention when Mr. Edward Snowden revealed that the NSA was spying on people from other nations because they had access to user's personal information due to the user's data being stored in the US). Based on the "Transparency and choice" section of GPP, it appears that the user is at the advantage of what is being shared to others, and to Google itself (the servers and administrators), and to companies other than Google. But, under closer examination, due to the use of the words 'can' and 'may', it appears Google is at the advantage, because they have the ability to prevent user's from accessing certain services if they do not allow Google to collect information (e.g. if users do not allow the use of cookies, some Google services cannot be accessed by the user due to the 'reason' that the service would not function properly).

Another issue of GPP is with the powers of domain administrators is that they have complete access to a user's Google account. It is a risk to users due to the administrator has the power to restrict users from deleting or editing their information, which can be seen as problematic because old information can do more harm to users (e.g. old friend affiliations may effect a person's employment due to the idea of guilty by association). A further dilemma in GPP lies if Google decides to merge, as the policy does not inform user's how the company would "ensure the confidentiality of any personal information" and does not allow users to opt out of the transferring of their information to another company and subject to a different private policy ("Privacy Policy – Privacy & Terms – Google"). GPP additionally does not discuss how the company guards against illegitimate access to it systems, which is problematic because the user does not know how their privacy is being protected. In addition, Google states that Google makes sure they comply with their private policy, while also adhering to self-regulatory frameworks. These two issues are a problem because (i) Google's responsibility is reduced because there is not a separate body to review if Google is actually complying with its policy;

and (ii) a user does not actually know if Google complies with its privacy policy because the company does not readily make available its results on its own adherence to its policy. Lastly is the issue of how Google deals with privacy of the dead. GPP does not address what happens to a user's information once they are deceased, which is problematic because a family may not get proper closure if they are constantly being reminded of their deceased loved one and it may cost a fortune to remove the information due to Google being reluctant to delete the data because of the difficulty of it and for financial reasons (Google can make more money off of ad revenues if the person still 'exists' online).

Grounding the problem: GPP

What many users do not realize about Google's services is that even the smallest "disclosures can be aggregated, data-mined, and tied together across many sites and social groups" and a "person's real-world identity can … be determined with a relatively small amount" of information (Conti, 12-13)[4]. This leads to the concept of ***Data Doubles***[5]. On a basic level, Data Doubles are a proxy for us online, and is made based on our online footprint. They are significant because they are said to be a reflection on us as people, and have the potential, if data mined properly, be a reflection of future behavior. An example that best describes this is the curly fry phenomenon (CFP), which stated that those who favorited a certain item on Facebook (in this case curly fries) had high IQ's [Golbeck, Ted Talk]. This raises the issue of if Data Doubles are actually reflections of us. In relation to the example, we must question if all those who "like" curly fries are actually smart, or if just many intelligent people like curly fries. Chances are it is the second option, because liking a particular item does not necessarily equate to being smart. So the question remains – are Data Doubles actual reflections of us currently?

---

[4] See Appendix B on page 20 for more detail.
[5] See Appendix C on page 21 for more context.

The answer is that they can be, but not necessarily. Data Doubles can be reflective of users because repeated actions a user does online can indicate a habit, and this habit can indicate what the person actually likes. For example, if a person buys many comics from Amazon, Amazon can assume that said person likes comics (a reflection of a person), and will attempt to sell them comics they think the person may like through recommendations (a reflection of future behavior). The reason behind the not necessarily reasoning can be best expressed with *Goffman's Dramaturgical Model*[3], which states that people will act differently in different situations and who is (or is not) present. What this means is that people may act differently while online then what they actually do in their personal time (lie online to appear a certain way), which translates to Data Doubles not being reflective of users. The significance of these two points is that companies can make more money and sell more targeted products with more information on users. It is problematic because the more information a user inputs on cites like Google, the more information Google has at its disposal, which is precarious due to the information being collected can be used against a user in real life, such as: (i) not being able to find a job or being fired because of a post the user made; or (ii) not being able to a get higher education because of search history.

Many users may wish that their Data Doubles not be kept with Google, not be created at all (if possible), and/or permanently deleted, while Google may argue they need Data Doubles to 'help' better and increase their services. This raises a question – should Google be allowed to keep Data Doubles? Provided Data Doubles are not being exploited, given to other companies to handle, not made (and cannot be made) public, and sold to other companies for profit, then Google should have the ability to keep Data Doubles, but Google must also get consent from users before they use the data to improve its services to its users. The issue of exploitation of personal data is also a concern, because as previously stated, information can be very damaging to a person's life (e.g. losing their job), but if an employer is looking into a prospective employee, they should have a right to view the created Data Double if a doubt exists into information the prospective employee is giving to the employer. For this to occur though, users must be informed and agree to this. This leads to another concern – the ownership of Data Doubles. Google could make the argument that they own them because it is their algorithms that collects that data in the first place, and they need them to improve services for users, while users could make the argument that they should own the Data Doubles because it is their information to begin with, and often users have to input some information to use websites. Currently, it can be argued that Google owns Data Doubles, because they are ones currently exploiting the data. Data Doubles should be owned by users, because they are the ones who really create the Doubles to begin with – it is the information inputted into algorithms that create the Data Double, not the algorithms themselves. It is important to have users own Data Doubles because it gives them real choices to share information to others. By letting users control Data Doubles, it gives them similar rights to actual users. If Data Doubles are not given rights (which they currently are not), people's rights are diminished, because instead of innocent until proven guilty, people are assumed guilty until they prove otherwise due to needing to defend what their 'online selves' include. Additionally, due to Data Doubles not having rights, they are constantly being monitored by law enforcement for 'national security' reasons, which brings up the question of societies compliance of living in a Panopticonic internet world, in which users have no privacy (due to possibly being monitored), and must conform to a certain online behavior due to not knowing when they are being watched, while the real punishment for not conforming to the standard is jail, loss of a status (e.g. loss of a job) and/or shaming through labels (e.g. being labeled immoral by friends and family if it was found out a person watched porn).

Stemming from the Panopticonic internet world idea is the question: should there be an expectation of privacy on Google, especially with what we consider 'secret' or 'sensitive' information, while keeping in mind Data Doubles[6]? Theoretically speaking, user's should be given some right to privacy while using Google's products, such as credit card information, because it would protect users from fraud, and give them the *right to be left alone*[7] from unwanted ads, or mail that may surprise them; but based on a thorough reading of GPP, the answer to this question is no, users should not expect any privacy while using Google services, due to where the information is stored, how it is handled with third parties, and how information is collected, which will be discussed in depth in the next section of this paper. The last issue to be addressed in this section of the paper is an argument Paul Nemitz makes, stating that information we put on the internet could be perceived as people looking at us nakedly (Baker). Mr. Nemitz's argument has some basis, because with the amount of information and the content we choose to upload can be very personal (e.g. intimate photos), and can be compared to nudity because like the concept of our body, we as people like to 'hide' things due to perceived embracement, and we do not wish to air are dirty laundry (personal information and/or our bodies) to an international stage (Baker).

Judging GPP and Suggestions on Improvement

Based on what has been presented, it can be argued that GPP is ineffective in protecting user's privacy due to the many ways Google exploits the user's data through the ambiguities and conditions (through phrasing), which leaves the majority of the public's private data mined by or

---

[6] See Appendix C on page 21 for more context
[7] See Appendix D on page 22 for more discussion.

sold to other companies, and/or is made public through the wording of the policy. Although Google has some fault to this, people are also to blame because many do not consider the expense of providing what Google does for free (many user's would be unwilling to pay the true cost for Google's services, and the way Google compensates for this is by reducing the rights of users to make money). To make GPP better, in theory, all implications mentioned in this paper should be addressed and fixed to help increase privacy rights of user's. In practice, however, this is unrealistic because Google needs to make money off of consumers somehow, and if they do not exploit users, they must charge for their services. The consumers in the short run may be unhappy about this because Google may become a luxury, but in the long run, it would benefit them because privacy can be better maintained. In this writer's opinion, Google users should become informed of GPP and its updates to enhance their understanding of what rights they have on Google, and inform themselves what happens to personal information they give Google, so that they are more careful in what information they select to share. Additionally, "a framework for identifying and understanding privacy problems" needs to be created so that "courts and policymakers can better balance privacy considerations against countervailing interests" (Solove, 196).

Canadian Issues and GPP

In this section, it will be examined how **Bill C-51** may effect GPP if the legislation gets passed in its January 30, 2015, First Reading format[8]. The first issue lies with how much information the government will be able to collect in the name of 'security'. What this means is that people's privacy would be further reduced because in the Government's view, to catch potential 'terrorist', everyone must be watched because the populace is labeled as potential criminals. One of the ways the government will be carrying this out would be to "criminalize

---

[8] See Appendix E on pages 23 and 24 for more details on this Act.

speech in support of 'terrorism offences in general,' and includes no requirement that the speaker actually intends for a terrorism offence to be committed" (Stryker). This is problematic because it is unclear "what kinds of speech and protest activity may be considered threats to national security if the bill passes" and it is ambiguous to typical Canadians where the line is crossed with information they choose to post online (Stryker). For example, someone's online political activity may put them on Canada's no-fly list for 'supporting terrorism', and that said person will not know or have the right to know if they are on the list, and they could be potentially arrested for that information because Bill C-51 reduces the threshold to arrest someone for suspected terrorism (Stryker).

Conclusion

As previously stated, privacy may be important to individuals, but by not becoming informed by GPP and its updates, users will continually have their privacy encroached upon. On the other hand, Google can do a lot better job of informing users of its private policy, such as implementing some sort of knowledge-based quiz, or adding a link to its main page to make it more accessible. Also at fault are every countries privacy laws, in which do little or nothing to help user's personal data be deleted, data mined, given to law enforcement with limited thresholds and/or sold to other companies. In conclusion, all of society must change together before privacy is looked upon, implemented, and talked about meaningfully.

Appendixes

Appendix A: Synopsis of the Safe Harbor Agreement

The Safe Harbor Agreement can be summarized to the following:

An agreement established between the United States Department of Commerce and the European Union (E.U.) in November 2000 to regulate the way that U.S. companies export and handle the personal data (such as names and addresses) of European citizens. The agreement is a policy compromise set up in response to a European directive that differed from traditional business procedures for U.S. companies dealing with the E.U. In 1998, the E.U. established the *European Commission Directive on Data Protection*, which prohibited data transfer to non-European countries that did not adhere to stringent criteria. In effect, because the guidelines were very strict, they made it illegal to transfer most citizens' personal data outside of Europe. Safe Harbor stipulations require that: companies collecting personal data must inform people that the data is being gathered, and tell them what will be done with it; they must obtain permission to pass on the information to a third party; they must allow people access to the data gathered; data integrity and security must be assured; and a means of enforcing compliance must be guaranteed. The agreement establishes a framework for a compromise solution between U.S. and E.U. privacy procedures. All 15 member countries are subject to the agreement, which means that data transfers can proceed without requiring individual authorization. U.S. companies that don't join Safe Harbor must obtain authorization separately from each European country. E.U. organizations can check a list of U.S. companies that have joined the collective to ensure that the *Safe Harbor Privacy Principles* will be adhered to (Rouse).

Appendix B: How disclosure can be a risk

The following chart from Mr. Greg Conti's *Googling Security: How Much Does Google Know About You* best illustrates how a seemingly simple and innocent search turns into reduced privacy to average users (112).

Service	Example	Example Information Disclosure Risk
Books	Books Google Hacking	Reading interests.
Calculator	3.14159 x 5	Math skill level and education level.
Currency Conversion	10 USD to GBP	Travel destinations.
Definitions	Define: google	User's education level.
I'm feeling lucky	N/A	User's familiarity with a given search results.
Map	Map: NYC	Physical location, travel plans, locations of family and friends.
Movies	Movie: Enemy of the State	Age, politics, education level.
Stock Information	Stock: Goog	Investment portfolios.
Translation	[Translate this Page]	Languages the user understands.
Travel Information	Lax airport	User's travel plans.

Source: Search Box and Related Applications Google Provides, *Googling Security: How Much Does Google Know About You*, 2009, Print, Table 4-7.

Appendix C: Definitions

For the purposes of this essay, a Data Double will be defined as an online proxy for a specific user, made by multiple companies' algorithms that track the specific user's online activity, to render "our conscious and unconscious patterns into data sets" which informs companies like Google what "precisely they can sell" (Duhigg). Data Doubles can also inform these companies on who we are, and what we might be in decades to come, as it can be argued that Data Doubles are our 'real selves'. Secret information will be defined as "information that a person deliberately decides to hide from other people, and involves at least two people" (in this case, each individual relationship between the company Google and its users) [Kelly, 4]. It differs from privacy because "privacy connotes the expectation of being free from unsanctioned intrusion" while secrecy "involves active attempts to prevent such intrusion or leaks, and the secret keeper exerts this energy in part because he or she perceives that other people may have some claim to the hidden information" (Kelly, 4). Sensitive information will be defined as information that one does not wish to share with many or any people, and is wished to be protected against unwarranted disclosure. A user will be defined as a person who is an account holder of a website, either voluntarily (an actual account holder) or through default (a non-account person that companies store information on through a "proxy" account).

Goffman's Dramaturgical Model states that social interaction can be compared to a theatre, and people are the actors, each of them performing different roles (Crossman). Also,

> [t]he audience consists of other individuals who observe the role-playing and react to the performances. In social interaction, like in theatrical performances, there is a front region where the actors are on stage in from of an audience. There is also a back region, or back stage, where individuals can be themselves and get rid of their role or identity that they play when they are in front of others. In stage drama, as in everyday interactions, according to Goffman, there are three regions, each with different affects on an individual's performance: front stage, back stage, and off-stage. The front stage is where the actor formally performs and adheres to conventions that have meaning to the audience. The actor knows he or she is being watched and acts accordingly. When in the back stage, the actor may behave differently than when in front of the audience on the front stage. This is where the individual truly gets to be himself or herself and get rid of the roles that he or she play when they are in front of other people. (Crossman).

Appendix D: A Case Study on the Significance of the Right to be Left Alone – The Target Story

The right to be left alone is an idea that people have the right to privacy and not be bothered by other people. In the case of Google, it would be the right not to be bombarded by advertisements or receiving unwanted targeted advertising, and the right not have personal information be used as a spying tool on users. This is best illustrated with a case with Target, in which the following happened to a family:

> "My daughter got this in the mail!" he said [The father]. "She's still in high school, and you're sending her coupons for baby clothes and cribs? Are you trying to encourage her to get pregnant?" The manager [of Target] didn't have any idea what the man was talking about. He looked at the mailer. Sure enough, it was addressed to the man's daughter and contained advertisements for maternity clothing, nursery furniture and pictures of smiling infants. The manager apologized and then called a few days later to apologize again. On the phone, though, the father was somewhat abashed. "I had a talk with my daughter," he said. "It turns out there's been some activities in my house I haven't been completely aware of. She's due in August. I owe you an apology" (Hill).

This real-life scenario is problematic because it illustrates how targeted advertising can have devastating consequences on a family, and also illustrates the argument that privacy does not exist online because of how valuable the information is to companies like Google.

Appendix E: Bill C-51

Bill C-51, at a basic level can be summed up in four parts:

Part 1 enacts the *Security of Canada Information Sharing Act*, which authorizes Government of Canada institutions to disclose information to Government of Canada institutions that have jurisdiction or responsibilities in respect of activities that undermine the security of Canada. It also makes related amendments to other Acts.

Part 2 enacts the *Secure Air Travel Act* in order to provide a new legislative framework for identifying and responding to persons who may engage in an act that poses a threat to transportation security or who may travel by air for the purpose of committing a terrorism offence. That Act authorizes the Minister of Public Safety and Emergency Preparedness to establish a list of such persons and to direct air carriers to take any necessary actions to prevent the commission of such acts. In addition, that Act establishes powers and prohibitions governing the collection, use and disclosure of information in support of its administration and enforcement. That Act includes an administrative recourse process for listed persons who have been denied transportation in accordance with a direction from the Minister of Public Safety and Emergency Preparedness and provides appeal procedures for persons affected by any decision or action taken under that Act. That Act also specifies punishment for contraventions of listed provisions and authorizes the Minister of Transport to conduct inspections and issue compliance orders. Finally, this Part makes consequential amendments to the *Aeronautics Act* and the *Canada Evidence Act*.

Part 3 amends the *Criminal Code* to, with respect to recognizances to keep the peace relating to a terrorist activity or a terrorism offence, extend their duration, provide for new thresholds, authorize a judge to impose sureties and require a judge to consider whether it is desirable to include in a recognizance conditions regarding passports and specified geographic areas. With respect to all recognizances to keep the peace, the amendments also allow hearings to be conducted by video conference and orders to be transferred to a judge in a territorial division other than the one in which the order was made and increase the maximum sentences for breach of those recognizances. It further amends the *Criminal Code* to provide for an offence of knowingly advocating or promoting the commission of terrorism offences in general. It also provides a judge with the power to order the seizure of terrorist propaganda or, if the propaganda is in electronic form, to order the deletion of the propaganda from a computer system. Finally, it amends the *Criminal Code* to provide for the increased protection of witnesses, in particular of persons who play a role in respect of proceedings involving security information or criminal intelligence information, and makes consequential amendments to other Acts.

Part 4 amends the *Canadian Security Intelligence Service Act* to permit the Canadian Security Intelligence Service to take, within and outside Canada, measures to reduce threats to the security of Canada, including measures that are authorized by the Federal Court. It authorizes the Federal Court to make an assistance order to give effect to a warrant issued under that Act. It also creates new reporting requirements for the Service and requires the Security Intelligence Review Committee to review the Service's performance in taking measures to reduce threats to the security of Canada.

Part 5 amends Divisions 8 and 9 of Part 1 of the *Immigration and Refugee Protection Act* to, among other things,

(*a*) define obligations related to the provision of information in proceedings under that Division 9;

(*b*) authorize the judge, on the request of the Minister, to exempt the Minister from providing the special advocate with certain relevant information that has not been filed with the Federal Court, if the judge is satisfied that the information does not enable the person named in a certificate to be reasonably informed of the case made by the Minister, and authorize the judge to ask the special advocate to make submissions with respect to the exemption; and

(*c*) allow the Minister to appeal, or to apply for judicial review of, any decision requiring the disclosure of information or other evidence if, in the Minister's opinion, the disclosure would be injurious to national security or endanger the safety of any person.
("Bill C-51")

Appendix F: Nothing to Hide?: A critical examination

A common argument that many use in favor of deregulation is with the statement 'if you have nothing to hide, then you should not worry'. The first problem with this argument is that it assumes that information that people want private is bad – this is not necessarily the case, as Solove states "[s]urveillance ... can inhibit such activities such lawful activities as free speech, free association, and other First Amendment rights essential for democracy" (27). Another problem with this argument is the potential for abuse – should government allow all information to be revealed by corporations, it can allow for further abuse of users (citizens) information (such as revealing 'private' information in courts) (Solove, 27). A third problem that arises from this argument is the potential lack of transparency on how the data collected would be used – in a database for governments, users do not know (and will not know due to the 'national security' excuse) what information is being used and do not have the ability to correct the information should it be false or incorrect, which is problematic, as people could potentially go to jail without knowing why, creating an Orwellian style society (Solove, 28). In addition, online information does not fully reflect users as a whole and may create a distorted view of the person, which can cause harm to people (e.g. being thrown in jail) if information is not contextualized properly (Solove, 28). Finally, the nothing to hide argument conceives privacy as having a narrow definition, but in reality, privacy (as discussed above) is very ambiguous and has plurality (Solove, 32). When one examines this plurality, the nothing to hide argument's main premises begin to unravel.

Work Cited

Baker, Jennifer. "'You Have No Right To See Me Naked!' Suddenly, Everyone Wakes Up At The Google-EU Face-Off." *The Register*. 5 Nov. 2014. Web. 17 Jan. 2015. <http://www.theregister.co.uk/2014/11/05/right_to_be_forgotten_eu_panel/?mt=1421290522 288>.

"BILL C-51." *PARLIAMENT of CANADA*. PARLIAMENT of CANADA, 30 Jan. 2015. Web. 3 May 2015. <http://www.parl.gc.ca/HousePublications/Publication.aspx?Language=E&Mode=1&DocId=6932136&Col=1&File=4>.

Conti, Greg. *Googling Security: How Much Does Google Know about You?* Upper Saddle River: Addison-Wesley, 2009. 1-30, 97-138. Print.

Crossman, Ashley. "The Presentation of Self in Everyday Life." About Education. Web. 2 May 2015. <http://sociology.about.com/od/Works/a/Presentation-Of-Self-Everyday-Life.htm>.

Duhigg, Charles. "How Companies Learn Your Secrets." *The New York Times* 16 Feb. 2012. Web. 8 Dec. 2014. <http://www.nytimes.com/2012/02/19/magazine/shopping-habits.html?pagewanted=all&_r=1&>.

"Factsheet on the "Right to be Forgotten" Ruling (C131-12)." European Commissions. Web. 17 Jan. 2015. <http://ec.europa.eu/justice/data-protection/files/factsheets/factsheet_data_protection_en.pdf>.

Heisenberg, Dorothee. "Data Privacy: Setting the International Standard." *Negotiating Privacy: The European Union, The United States, and Personal Data Protection*. Boulder: Lynne Reiner, 2005. 1-24. Print.

Hill, Kashmir. "How Target Figured Out A Teen Girl Was Pregnant Before Her Father Did." *Forbes*. Forbes Magazine, 16 Feb. 2012. Web. 4 May 2015. <http://www.forbes.com/sites/kashmirhill/2012/02/16/how-target-figured-out-a-teen-girl-was-pregnant-before-her-father-did/>.

Keizer, Garret. "What Is Privacy and Are We Even Able to Say?" *Privacy*. New York: Picador, 2012. 14-23. Print.

Kelly, Anita E. "The Nature of Secrecy." *The Psychology of Secrets*. New York: Kluwer Academic/Plenum, 2002. 3-8. Print.

Kobzar, Dr. Olena. "Privacy Law in Canada: PIPEA." Privacy and the Law 3365 Lecture. York University. York University, Toronto. 12 Jan. 2015. Lecture.

"Privacy Policy – Privacy & Terms – Google." *Privacy Policy – Privacy & Terms – Google*. Google, 19 Dec. 2014. Web. 3 May 2015. <http://www.google.com/policies/privacy/>.

Rouse, Margaret. "What Is Safe Harbor? - Definition from WhatIs.com." *SearchCIO*. Web. 3 May 2015. <http://searchcio.techtarget.com/definition/Safe-Harbor>.

Solove, Daniel J. *Understanding Privacy*. Cambridge, Mass.: Harvard UP, 2008. 1-11, 171-198. Print.

Solove, Daniel J. "The Nothing-to-Hide Argument." *Nothing to Hide: The False Tradeoff between Privacy and Security*. New Haven, Conn.: Yale UP, 2011. 23-32. Print.

Stryker, Alyssa. "8 Things You Need to Know about Bill C-51." *BC Civil Liberties Association 8 Things You Need to Know about Bill C51 Comments*. BCCLA, 11 Mar. 2015. Web. 3 May 2015. <https://bccla.org/2015/03/8-things-you-need-to-know-about-bill-c-51/>.

The Curly Fry Conundrum: Why Social Media "likes" Say More than You Might Think. Ted Talks, 2014. Film.

Vistila, Miia, and Floora Ruokonen. "Social Networking Sites and Privacy as Contextual Integrity." *Revealing Privacy Debating the Understandings of Privacy*. Ed. Margherita Carucci. Frankfurt Am Main: Peter Lang, 2012. 119-132. Print.